ARE YOU FIRED UP OR BURNED OUT?

JAMES W. MOORE

Abingdon Press / *Nashville*

Other books by James W. Moore

Yes, Lord, I Have Sinned, but I Have Several Excellent Excuses
Seizing the Moments
Attitude Is Your Paintbrush
Some Folks Feel the Rain...Others Just Get Wet
Daddy, Is That Story True, or Were You Just Preaching?
Christmas Gifts That Won't Break
Bethlehem or Bedlam?

Library of Congress Cataloging-in-Publication Data

Names: Moore, James W. (James Wendell), 1938-
Title: Are you fired up or burned out? / James W. Moore.
Description: First [edition]. | Nashville, Tennessee : Abingdon Press, 2016.
Identifiers: LCCN 2015036672 | ISBN 9781501816628 (binding: pbk.)
Subjects: LCSH: Christian life.
Classification: LCC BV4501.3 .M6549 2016 | DDC 248.4—dc23 LC record available at http://lccn.loc.gov/2015036672

17 18 19 20 21 22—10 9 8 7 6 5 4 3 2 1

MANUFACTURED IN THE UNITED STATES OF AMERICA

Contents

Introduction / v

1. Are You Fired Up or Burned Out? / 1

2. Can You Finish Strong? / 9

3. Christ Is the Answer, but What Are the Questions? / 13

4. Do You Have "Christed Eyes"? / 17

5. Do You Use Time Creatively? / 21

6. Do You Have a Faith That Will Not Shrink? / 25

7. When Is Stubbornness a Good Thing? / 29

8. What Is the Best Tribute We Can Pay Our Lord? / 33

9. Why Is Gratitude So Important? / 37

10. What's the Difference Between Childishness and Childlikeness? / 41

11. Do You Build Walls or Bridges? / 45

12. Have You Ever Experienced God's Surprising, Reconciling Presence? / 49

Contents

13. Are You Talking More and Communicating Less? / 53

14. Do You Love Anyone Like That? / 57

15. Did Jesus Really Mean That? / 61

16. When God Speaks, Can the Church Be Our
Hearing Aid? / 65

17. Do You Know Firsthand the Grace of God that Sets Us
Free? / 69

18. Is Jesus God's Way of Getting Rid of a Bad
Reputation? / 73

19. Anybody Here Enjoy Religion? / 77

20. Do You Make Excuses, Excuses, Excuses? / 81

21. Are You Standing In the Need of Prayer? / 85

22. What Shall I Do to Inherit Eternal Life? / 89

23. Do You Really Know the Good News? / 93

24. What Are the Most Authentic Qualities of Life? / 97

25. Are You Dreaming the Impossible Dream? / 101

26. Are You Locked in a Room with Open Doors? / 105

27. Was the Innkeeper Really a Bad Guy? / 109

28. Where's His? / 113

29. Will You Face Death Unafraid? / 117

Bibliography / 121

Introduction

I saw him coming. I could tell that he was troubled, bur-dened, despondent. His body language spoke volumes. His shoulders were dramatically slumped as if he were carrying the weight of the world on his back. He walked as if his shoes were filled with lead, trudging along, one heavy footstep after another.

He came to the door of my office, paused for a brief moment, and then plodded on in and slumped tiredly into the chair across from my desk. I walked around the desk, sat next to him, and asked, "Are you all right?"

"No," he said dejectedly. "I am worn out, world-weary to the depth of my bones, and stressed to the max!"

"Do you want to talk about it?" I asked.

He said, "I'm just so tired of the daily grind. I love my wife, I love my children, my job's OK, but the excitement is gone. I feel like I'm running up a hill and I can't get to the top. Everything in my life has just grown so stale and monotonous.

"It wasn't always like this," he added. "I used to celebrate life, but now all I do is cope!"

That man in my office that day spoke out loud about the world-weariness that many people feel these days.

This sense of boredom, futility, melancholy, and tiredness that settles on the human spirit is a tragic characteristic of life in our hectic, frenzied, stressful, modern world. The sad truth is that while we have done so well and have been so creative in so many dimensions of life, we have all too often missed the main thing. We have moved into outer space, but we have not really discovered and celebrated the mysteries and wonders of our own inner space.

I am writing this book because I am convinced that life does not have to be boring or monotonous or tiresome. I believe with all my heart that God meant life to be celebrative, zestful, meaningful, and joyful. I believe with all my heart that God wants us to be fired up about life, not burned out.

The truth is that this world-weariness that plagues us is not so much the problem as it is a symptom of a much deeper problem called emptiness. It's the emptiness that comes from loving and craving the wrong things…temporal, material things that will never satisfy. We scrape and scramble to get them, only to discover that they don't fill the vacuum. Then we feel cheated, shortchanged, let down, bored, empty, and bone-weary.

But, it doesn't have to be that way! God does not want it to be that way for us. Jesus came that we might have exciting, joyful, abundant life!

In the pages that follow, we will take a look at some ways, with God's help and God's grace and Jesus' life and teaching, that we can stay excited, exhilarated, fulfilled, and fired up about life.

Are You Fired Up or Burned Out?

Let me ask you an intensely personal question: Are you fired up or burned out? These two phrases, *fired up* and *burned out*, are popular expressions that we are hearing more and more these days. On the one hand, we walk into a basketball arena or a football stadium and we hear the fans cheering with a primitive rhythm: "Get fired up.... Get fired up!" Or we hear a college student who has just been invited to the homecoming dance by that someone special say excitedly, "I'm fired up!"

To be fired up is to be excited, optimistic, hopeful, confident, courageous, energetic. To be fired up is to be glad to be alive and enthusiastic about living. To be fired up is to say an emphatic, celebrative *yes!* to life and its wonderful possibilities and opportunities.

Recently, I heard about Willie, age five, whose father took him to his first football game. Willie took it all in. And that night, to the amazement and amusement of his parents, he said his prayers with true football snap: "God bless Mama, God bless Daddy, God bless Willie, rah, rah, rah." Willie had gotten fired up.

However, another expression has worked its way into the jargon of our time. We call it *burnout*. To be burned out is to be tired, exhausted, worn down, disillusioned, disappointed, and depleted. To be burned out is to be discouraged and pessimistic and ready to throw in the towel. To be burned out is to be filled with dread and drudgery and emptiness.

In this frantic, busy world, we can relate to burnout, and we can identify with the Red Queen's words to Alice in Wonderland that "it takes all the running you can do to keep in the same place. If you want to get somewhere else, you must run at least twice as fast as that!" Be sure to notice that burnout can happen to anyone. You don't have to be a corporate executive to have this problem. It can come to anyone, and it does. Burnout is related, I think, to disillusionment. It's the fatigue and frustration brought on by devotion to a cause or a job or a way of life—or a relationship—that failed to produce the expected reward. A person tries and tries and tries, and then feels let down, depleted, exhausted, disenchanted. Where once there was the feeling of being fired up, now there is the tired, aching sense of being burned out.

Although the word *burnout* seems new to us, the experience is actually quite old. There are several references to it in the Scriptures. Take, for example, the experience of Elijah. He was a prophet in a time of real testing in ancient Israel. Jezebel, the pagan queen of Ahab, the king of Israel, had introduced idolatry to the land. This was a flagrant violation of the First Commandment. Pagan gods were worshiped in Israel because of Jezebel. God's temple was profaned because of Jezebel. Priests were murdered because of Jezebel. Elijah spoke out against these idolatrous practices. He challenged Jezebel's priests to a contest to determine the one true God: Jehovah or Baal. Elijah won the contest on Mount Carmel. He showed up Jezebel's priests, but in so doing he aroused the vengeful wrath of Jezebel. Then, worn out physically, depleted emotionally, tired, and scared, Elijah experienced burnout. Negative reactions set in. He lost his confidence and his courage. He ran away. His despair was so deep that he wanted to die. "It's more than enough," he cried to the Lord. "Take my life because I'm no better than my ancestors" (1 Kings 19:4). Then, feeling alone, he whined, "I'm the only one left" (v. 10). But go on and read the rest of the story. It is an amazing account of spiritual therapy and the resurgence of faith. There, in the desert, he found physical renewal. He enjoyed a change of scenery. There, he heard the still, small voice of God. And he began to see a glimmer of hope, and he was able to take up the torch again.

Some years later, a young prophet named Isaiah went through similar feelings. As he struggled with his despair, he found God, and he wrote some words that will live forever: "[God gives] power to the tired and [revives] the exhausted" (Isaiah 40:28-29). In addition to that powerful verse of Scripture, I'll list three more things that will help avoid burnout.

First, *recognize your fatigue limit.* Some years ago, I ran across an article that lifted up three visual symbols—three household items—that can help you recognize your fatigue limit: a piece of wire, a rubber band, and an electric fuse. Think of a piece of wire. Mechanical engineers, who study the strength of metals, know that every metal has a fatigue limit. For example, you might take a stiff piece of wire and bend it repeatedly and vigorously one hundred times, and maybe nothing happens. But then on the one hundred first time the wire is bent, the wire may snap like a brittle twig. Eventually the wire will have passed its fatigue limit.

Does that sound like your life? You go along, facing crisis after crisis, and you hang tough. Then one day you are "bent" one time too many, and something snaps. And you are no longer in control. You have passed your fatigue limit. The fatigue limit for us is that point when our personality goes to pieces, we lose our capacity for self-management and self-control, and we snap.

Next, think of a rubber band. You can stretch it and stretch it, but if you stretch it too much, it sags. It loses its resiliency. Its vibrancy vanishes. It can't bounce back anymore. That's its fatigue limit. When it doesn't have the strength to bounce back to its original form, it has passed its limit.

Or think of an electric fuse. If you overload the circuits, the fuse will blow. And when we demand too much of ourselves, we may blow a fuse. We need to be aware of what our fatigue limits are and live within them. Here are some practical tests: if we are sleeping too little or too much, if we are eating too little or too much, if we are talking too little or too much, if we are daydreaming too little or too much, if we are feeling afraid of people, if we see every task as a chore filled with drudgery, if we have lost our sense of humor, if we have lost excitement in our work, if we feel unable to pray, then we may be approaching our fatigue limit.

Second, *remember your priorities.* Much of our nervous tension that leads to burnout comes from mixed-up priorities, from our failure to see what matters and what does not. Someone has said we are guilty of "frittered living." We spend our lives "toying with trifles" and thus are not prepared for the big demands life will make. We need to learn to ignore the insignificant and concentrate on the vital.

Back in 1949, the name Joe Page was known to all baseball fans. He was a relief pitcher for the New York Yankees. To put it better, he was one of the greatest relief pitchers in the history of baseball. Smoking Joe Page was at his best in the most pressure-packed situations. When the bases were loaded, with nobody out and the game at stake in the last inning, that's when they would bring Joe in from the bullpen. He would take the mound relaxed and poised. His presence steadied the whole team. His confidence gave new confidence to his teammates. When asked how he could be so calm in such tense situations, Joe gave a fascinating answer. He said he had learned to ignore what did not matter: He paid no attention to the men on base. He was concerned with only one thing: getting the batter out. The men on base could not hurt him so long as he could get the batter out. That was his priority. He had learned to ignore what did not matter.

That reminds me of an old poem:

> One ship drives east and another drives
>   west,
> With the selfsame winds that blow;

'Tis the set of the sails and not the gales,
Which tell us the way to go.
Like the winds of the sea are the winds
   of fate,
As we voyage along through life;
'Tis the set of the soul that decides its
   goal,
And not the calm or the strife.

                —Ella Wheeler Wilcox

We need to recognize our fatigue limit; we need to remember our priorities.

And finally, *relax your soul in God.* Wallace Hamilton said it well: "Nothing takes the fear out of life so much as an awareness deep within of God's nearness and His loving concern."

Many years ago, hymn writer Kathrina von Schlegel felt that too, and she wrote these beautiful words:

Be still, my soul; the Lord is on thy side;
Bear patiently the cross of grief or pain;
Leave to thy God to order and provide;
In every change He faithful will remain.
Be still, my soul; thy best, thy heavenly,
   Friend
Through thorny ways leads to a joyful
   end.

God is with us. God is on our side. Now that's something to get fired up about! Remember how Isaiah put it: "[God gives] power to the tired and revives the weak."

Red is the color of Pentecost because one of the key symbols for the Spirit of God is the flame. The message is clear. When God's flame is in us, when God's spirit is in us, we will be fired up. But when we shut God's flame out of our lives, when we shut God's Spirit out of our lives, we might burn out.

2

Can You Finish Strong?

When I was in high school, I enjoyed running track. I was a sprinter for the team at Tech High in Memphis, and I ran the 100- and 220-yard dashes and also did some field events such as the long jump.

But more than anything, I liked being on the sprint relay teams. There was something very special to me about being a part of a team: that camaraderie, that spirit, that closeness that comes from working together like a well-tuned, synchronized machine; that unique fellowship that comes from winning and losing together, from rejoicing and hurting together, from laughing and crying together.

We had a good 880-yard relay team. Each runner would run 220 yards, hand the baton at full speed to the next man who would then run his leg of the race and hand the baton to the next man until all four runners had completed the 880-yard distance.

We had a fine team and we came through all of our meets undefeated until the day of the regional track meet. All we had to do was finish in the top three to win a trip to the state meet in Knoxville.

Earlier in the season we had defeated every team in the race. We were confident—maybe even a bit cocky. We had already made plans for our trip to Knoxville. Then came time for the race, the 880-yard relay.

We were primed and ready. Our first runner jumped out front and got us a good lead. Our second runner increased it. I was next and when I passed the baton to our anchor man, we had a forty-yard lead.

As I stood and watched our last runner coming out of the final turn—way out in front—I began to think about the medals we were going to win, the trophy that would be placed in the trophy case at school with our names on it, our pictures in the paper, the trip to Knoxville, and the opportunity to run in the state track meet.

Suddenly, I was brought back to reality. Our anchor man, just 35 yards short of the finish, pulled a muscle and fell down. As he lay there, holding his leg, writhing in pain, one by one, the other teams passed him. Instead of finishing in first place, we came in last.

Just that quickly, it was all over. I can remember, as if it were yesterday, the sick feeling in the pit of my stomach, the concern and empathy for my injured teammate, and the pain over our lost opportunity.

But I learned a valuable lesson about life that day. I learned dramatically how important it is to finish what you start. It's not enough to make a good start. It's not enough to just run well. It's not enough to wow the crowd. You have to finish. You have to see it through or it is all to no avail.

Harry Emerson Fosdick said it well.

> A very serious test of human fiber is involved in the fact that there are so many good beginnings and poor endings.
>
> ...Good starters and good stayers are not necessarily the same people. Ardor, excitement, susceptibility to sudden feeling, the flare of good intentions—such forces set men going, but they do not enable men to carry on when the going is hard. That requires another kind of moral energy which evidently is not so common as the first. Plenty of people...get away easily. They are off with fleet eagerness..., but they peter out; they soon stick in the sand or stall on a high hill.
>
> ...In one of our Federal prisons today is a man who for fifty years with unblemished reputation lived a life of probity and honor in his own community. Then, as a government servant, he went to France during the war and mishandled funds. Only that will be remembered about him. The half century of fine living is blotted out. He was not able to finish.

The great people of history were persons with power to see it through. Albert Einstein, Winston Churchill, Abraham Lincoln, Thomas Edison, Helen Keller—all had reasons to quit, but they didn't.

Through determination and commitment, they persisted, endured, persevered. Against this backdrop, the words of Jesus ring out even more powerfully as we see him hanging there on a cross and saying with his last breath, "It is finished. I have seen it through."

3

Christ Is the Answer, but What Are the Questions?

Some years ago, the *Houston Chronicle* ran a story about a test given to some music students in an unidentified junior high school. Here are some of their interesting answers:

- "Music sung by two people at the same time is called a 'duel'."
- "I know what a sextet is...but I had rather not say!"
- "A xylophone is an instrument used mainly to illustrate the letter X."
- "Dirges are music written to be played at sad, sad occasions, such as funerals, weddings, and the like."
- "Refrain means 'don't do it!' A refrain in music is the part you better not try to sing."

- "A virtuoso is a musician with real high morals."
- "J. S. Bach died from 1750 to the present."
- "Handel was half German, half Italian and half English....He was rather large!"

Now, we can tell from the results of this one music test that right answers are important. But have you stopped to think that the right questions are important too?

How essential it is to get the right answers matched with the right questions! Nowhere is this more true than in the realm of religion. It is common to see bumper stickers, posters, buttons, and highway signs displaying the words "Christ is the answer." Of course, as Christians we believe this to be true. We believe that Christ is the answer, that he is the highest revelation of what God is like and what God wants us to be like.

Isn't that what the word *revelation* means? A disclosure, an unfolding, new light, new meaning, new understanding? But the words "Christ is the answer" must be more than religious cliché or pious platitude.

The serious student or thinker comes back and asks, "If Christ is the answer, what are the questions?" The only way any answer can be relevant and meaningful for us is to relate that answer to the proper question.

Math books sometimes have answers printed in the back. You can always get the right answer, but the answers by themselves mean nothing. They become significant and meaningful only when they are related to the specific problems given in the lessons of the textbook. Only then do learning and growth occur. It isn't enough to just know the answer. You have to also know the question.

"Christ is the answer," but what are the questions? The noted psychologist Erik Erikson says there are five basic developmental questions that every person must ask and answer creatively before that person can become "whole" or "mature."

Christ came to bring us wholeness, to make us whole, the Scriptures tell us. Similar to the questions Erikson raises, we will look at how Christ brings light and meaning and answers to five basic questions that every person must answer before he or she can have full, abundant life.

1. Identity: "Who am I?"
2. Intimacy: "Who am I in relation to others?"
3. Faith: "Why am I here?"
4. Loyalty: "To whom and to what will I be true?"
5. Vocation: "What is my uniqueness or special calling?"

These were the questions the prodigal son grappled with, and they are the questions every person must ask and answer before he or she can have real life.

Christ helps us answer these questions, and the answer is good news. He tells us that we are the beloved and valued children of God, that God claims us as children and loves us like the gracious father in the prodigal son parable.

We are God's beloved children, related to all other people as brothers and sisters in his family. We are family, and we should live together in love and harmony and with respect and understanding. We are here to share this good news that God cares and wants us to be caring.

We are here to love God and love people. We are here to serve and trust and be loyal to God even when times are hard. Our challenge is to discover—with God's help—our own unique gifts and to use these special gifts as best we can to continue the ministry of love that Christ began.

4

Do You Have "Christed Eyes"?

From the story of the rich young ruler in the Gospel of Mark (10:17-22), we can learn in a backdoor kind of way the key characteristics of Christian discipleship and, more precisely, what it means to be Christian or "Christlike."

Jesus is on the way to Jerusalem (and the cross) when the rich young ruler runs up and kneels before him. He runs up (a sign of enthusiasm); he kneels down (a sign of respect and reverence). We can assume that this young man is not trying to trap Jesus with loaded questions (as others tried), but that he is really sincere when he asks, "Good Teacher, what must I do to obtain eternal life?"

Jesus answers, "You know the commandments: Don't commit murder. Don't commit adultery. Don't steal. Don't give false testimony....Honor your father and mother."

Then the young man responds: "I've kept all these things since I was a boy."

Jesus then looks at him with love and says to him: "You are lacking one thing. Go, sell what you own, and give the money to the poor. Then you have treasure in heaven. And come, follow me" (Mark 10:17, 19-21). At this, the rich young ruler turns away and leaves sorrowfully, for he is a wealthy man.

Here in the rich young ruler's failure to respond and follow, we find some basic insights into what it means to be Christian. Here are a few; you will think of others.

First, a Christian is one who sees God through the eyes of Christ. That's the key thing about Jesus. He shows us what God is like. He gives God a face, and that face is love. John Killinger put it like this: "Jesus is God's way of getting rid of a bad reputation!" Jesus came to show us that God is not an angry and hostile deity, not an impersonal cosmic force, but a loving father, a God of love and compassion who cares for all of his children. We don't have to be afraid of God, or of life and its problems or challenges, because God is with us to see us through them. The rich young ruler didn't understand this and, frightened, he turned away.

Second, a Christian is one who sees value through the eyes of Christ. In the rich young ruler incident, Christ gives us a new way of looking at things, a new way of measuring what is important.

Sometimes we stress the rich young ruler's lack of commitment so much that we miss one of the key insights of this story, namely, Christ's way of measuring what's valuable!

The rich young ruler is a success. He has it all: wealth, youth, power—and yet there is something lacking, an emptiness, a hunger. Jesus sees right to the heart of it. He is not criticizing wealth. Rather, he is saying, "Following me is the greatest treasure in the world. It is wealth beyond counting." Here Jesus is talking not just about the cost of discipleship, but about the *riches* of discipleship, and he is saying that discipleship is better than dollars. It's the most valuable thing in the world.

Third, a Christian is one who sees other people through the eyes of Christ. The overriding keynote of Christ's life and ministry was concern and love for other people. This love for others is underscored in the rich young ruler story. Christ tells the young man to care for the poor and needy, and when they talk about the commandments, they mention only those that deal with our relationships with other people. There's no mention of love for God here. Why? Because this is the way we express our love for God best—by loving other people! A friend of mine once said, "When I first became a Christian, I was so excited that I wanted to hug God. Over the years, I have learned that the way you hug God is to hug people!"

And fourth, a Christian is one who sees life through the eyes of Christ. When we look at life through the eyes of Christ, two things stand out: urgency and self-giving. The rich young ruler missed that. Yet this is what Jesus had in mind when he said, "The Kingdom is at hand"; that is, "Now is the time to serve the King of kings!" We could well describe Christ's life as "urgent self-givingness." He saw every moment as a unique and urgent opportunity to give himself for others.

That's what it means to be a Christian: serving God and giving ourselves for the cause of Christ in every moment; seeing every day, every occasion as an opportunity to serve God in a Christlike way...in other words, to have "Christed Eyes."

5

Do You Use Time Creatively?

Some time ago, a good friend of mine died. She was a great woman who had been a saint in the church for more than eighty years. I went to her funeral and had an interesting experience there.

In the funeral service, two ministers spoke and, coincidentally, used the same biblical text. Psalm 90:12: "Teach us to number our days so we can have a wise heart." It was interesting that both had selected this text, but what was even more remarkable was that their interpretations of the verse were so dramatically different. In fact, they were almost exact opposites.

The first minister stepped into the pulpit and said:

> This verse, "Teach us to number our days so we can have a wise heart," is so appropriate for this service of commemoration because

the one whose life we celebrate here in this
funeral service was an embodiment of this
text. She lived it out!

She saw time as a precious and valuable
gift from God. She saw every day as a new,
fresh opportunity to serve God and his truth
and will. She used her days, she numbered
her days, to get a heart of deep, spiritual
wisdom.

Then the second minister stepped into the pulpit and said
something totally different: "This verse, 'Teach us to number
our days so we can have a wise heart,' simply means you better wise up because your days are numbered!"

So we see two ministers speaking in the same service on
the same text, but coming out with two drastically different
ideas as to its meaning. Not only that, but we see here in their
contrasting views two different understandings of time.

The first man saw time as a valuable gift, each day a
unique opportunity for new wisdom and new service. The
second man saw time as an enemy, a battlefield to be saved
from, a testing period.

The first man saw time as a friend, an ally to be lived
enthusiastically and optimistically. The second man saw time
as a period of preparation for something to come, almost like
a prisoner "x-ing" off the days on the calendar in his cell, a
period covered with dread and temptation and pessimism.

This reminded me of an old story describing the difference
between a pessimist and an optimist. The pessimist wakes
up in the morning, opens his eyes, and says, "Good Lord, it's

morning!" whereas the optimist wakes up in the morning, opens his eyes, and says, "Good morning, Lord!"

When I got back to my office after my friend's funeral, I saw that someone had put a magazine clipping on my desk. It was a news story about four San Francisco teenagers who had gone on a rampage, driving through the crowded streets in a speeding car, throwing bricks and rocks at innocent bystanders. Several people were injured, some critically.

The boys were caught and were asked, "Why?" They said, "We were bored! We didn't have anything else to do. We were just killing time."

There in a short period, I had been exposed to three different concepts of time:

- One saw time as a precious gift from God.
- One saw time as a testing period full of dread.
- One group of teenage boys saw time as something to be killed or wasted, to be used up while waiting for some fortune to fall in their laps.

What about you? Where do you fit in? How do you view and use time?

One thing is sure. Our understanding of time affects every fiber of our being. Our concept of time affects our theology, our morality, our emotions, our work, our family, our personal life, as well as our relationship with God and with other people.

The psalmist realized this when he said, "Teach us to number our days." Wasn't he really saying, "Lord, teach us how to use our time creatively!"

Of course, Jesus was a master at this. Author Charlie Shedd had some helpful words about this:

> When we study Jesus and his days on Earth and the way He used His time, we are overcome with awe. Given no more than three years of actual recorded ministry, He split history in two sections—"before" and "after" His own time.
>
> In this brief span, He gathered to Himself a motley group and fashioned a force for building a world kingdom. He preached sermons, taught lessons, said things which have become the theme of several thousands of books. He established a church, wrought a world kingdom, had time for "even the least," and kept great blocks of time for nothing but pure communion with the Father.
>
> We do well to relive His life as nearly as we can and repeatedly ask ourselves, "What could He do with these minutes and hours if He were living in me today?"

How do we use time creatively? As has been suggested, we use time creatively by living life in the spirit of Christ.

6

Do You Have a Faith That Will Not Shrink?

O for a faith that will not shrink" an old hymn goes. The hymn writer knew the problem that many people have in their spiritual experience.

It happens far too much. People have a meaningful faith experience. For several weeks or months or even years, all goes well. They become excited, enthusiastic, devoted. Every time the church doors open up to them, they are there and it's all wonderful.

But then suddenly, they begin to have problems. They begin to drop out. The luster wears off. The excitement wears thin. The enthusiasm wears out. The devotional commitment shrinks.

And then after a while, they disappear and become not much more than vague names on some church roll. No one sees them at the church anymore. No one really seems to know them anymore.

Why does this happen? And how can we prevent it? How can we keep our spiritual experience vibrant? How can we keep our faith alive and well? We can find some fascinating and helpful clues in (of all places) the garden of Gethsemane. Ironically, as we look closely at Jesus facing physical death, we find the keys to staying alive.

Consider four ingredients of a lively, healthy faith.

To Keep Our Faith Alive, We Must Continue to Pray

Jesus was a man of prayer. We notice in the Gospels that he often "went apart" to pray. It was his way of communing with God. So we are not surprised when he falls on his knees in the garden of Gethsemane. Prayer was his means of keeping his faith alive. It kept him in touch with God, and because of it, he was able to do what he had to do.

To Keep Our Faith Alive, We Must Continue to Grow and Learn

In the garden of Gethsemane, Jesus was open to new truth. His mind was working overtime: straining, stretching, struggling. He didn't say, "Now, see here. This is the way it is and there is no other way!"

No, he was open to God's truth; to God's will; to God's direction.

Being a disciple means being a "learner." Too often and too quickly, people forget that.

There's a story about a little boy who fell out of bed one night. He said, "I guess I fell asleep too close to where I first got in!" This can happen to us. As soon as we stop studying and learning and growing in the faith, at that moment our faith begins to shrivel and fade, shrink and die. We are like plants...we need light—the Light—to grow.

To Keep Our Faith Alive, We Must Continue to Obey God

When Jesus left the garden of Gethsemane, he went out to face the cross. He didn't want to do it. That was not his first choice. He struggled against it. He agonized over it. But he did it!

He knew that he must stand tall for what is right. He knew that he must not run away. He knew that he had to strike a blow for God's justice...even if it meant death on a cross. To keep our faith alive, we need that kind of come-what-may obedience.

To Keep Our Faith Alive, We Must Have the Determination to Stay with It, No Matter What

In the garden of Gethsemane, Jesus had every reason to drop out. It would have been easy to throw in the towel, but he would not quit. He had made up his mind to do the best he knew...and to trust God to bring it out right. Later, on the cross, he said, "Father, into your hands I entrust my life" (Luke 23:46).

Keeping our faith alive takes determination and perseverance...and a lot of trust!

7

When Is Stubbornness a Good Thing?

Is stubbornness ever a virtue? We do not usually include stubbornness in our list of virtuous qualities. On the contrary, we most often list it as a vice, equating it with closed-mindedness or mule-headedness.

If the symbol of peace is the descending dove, then the symbol of stubbornness is the balking mule.

A husband and wife, while on an automobile trip, got into an argument over a small-sized incident. Neither would budge. Neither would listen. Neither would give an inch. Each loudly and stubbornly argued for his or her position with neither giving in or backing down. The heated debate was followed by a cold, stony silence. For miles they didn't speak.

Finally, they passed a pasture where a young farm boy was trying to pull a long-eared mule across a narrow, makeshift bridge. The mule balked. He did not budge. And even though the boy pulled with all his might, the mule was not about to move. The mule had dug in its heels. Seeing this, the husband broke the silence. "Look at that stubborn old mule!" he said. Then, pointing to the mule, he asked his wife, "Is that stubborn old mule a relative of yours?"

The wife retorted: "Yes, on my husband's side!"

This is a light treatment of the heavy notion that we have about stubbornness; namely, that stubbornness usually does not make a pretty picture. Most often, stubbornness is narrow, rigid, arrogant, unyielding, prideful, unbending, difficult to live with, and hard to handle. In Merriam-Webster's Dictionary, the synonym is "obstinate," meaning "perversely adhering to an opinion." That is the portrait of stubbornness with which we are most familiar.

But in one of the most fascinating and refreshing sections in all the Scriptures, the Apostle Paul shows us in his Letter to the Philippians that there also is a virtuous kind of stubbornness, a "sanctified stubbornness," a consecrated, tenacious determination to hold on and persevere no matter how dark and dismal the circumstances.

Facing frustrating troubles, physical dangers, debilitating circumstances, and incredible odds, Paul stubbornly refuses to sell out or give in or fold.

Sometimes, as people of faith, when we run head-on into trials, troubles, or temptations, we are called on to express a "sanctified Christian stubbornness"! There is much to learn from the Apostle Paul on this subject:

- He stubbornly refused to give in to self-pity.
- He stubbornly refused to be shaken by criticism.

- He stubbornly refused to quit on life.
- He stubbornly refused to compromise on his commitment to God.

That kind of stubbornness is virtuous indeed. We could all use some of that, couldn't we?

8

What Is the Best Tribute We Can Pay Our Lord?

My father died as the result of an automobile accident when I was twelve years old. It was on a Sunday afternoon. He had appendicitis and was being rushed to the hospital when the accident occurred. We walked the floors of the hospital and prayed in the chapel for several hours before we were sent home for the night.

Shortly after my brother, my sister, and I had fallen asleep, the call came from the hospital that my father had died. Even though I was only twelve, I have several very vivid images of that tragic event in our lives.

When the call came about my father's death, the relatives who had gathered decided to let the children sleep. They felt it best to let us get a good night's rest and then tell us the next morning. But what they didn't count on was that I got up early and went out to get the morning paper. When I opened it up, there on the front page was the picture of our smashed-up car and the announcement that my dad had died as a result of the car wreck. Before anyone could tell me, I read it in the paper.

I remember as if it were yesterday. I was sitting in the living room of our home early that morning with the relatives coming in and seeing me there and not knowing what to say. And I remember feeling sorry for them.

Another vivid image is from that night at the funeral home. As we stood there by my father's casket, scores and scores of people came by...all different kinds of people. Some were rich and some were poor; some were young and some were old; some were black, some were white, and some were Asian; some were professional people and some were uneducated laborers; some I knew quite well and some I had never seen before. But they all came. They came over and spoke to us and expressed their sympathy. And almost every one of them said to me the same thing: "Jim, your dad was kind to me."

I determined then and there that the best tribute I could pay to my dad was to take up his torch of kindness, and from that moment on I have tried to be a kind person. I haven't always succeeded, but I have tried and I am still trying to let my father's kindness live on in me.

Think about that and think about what a kind person Jesus was. We give up on people. We write them off. We conclude that there is no hope for them. We decide that they are beyond redemption. But Jesus never did that. He was kind to the end. He never relinquished his loving-kindness. Even on the cross, he was taking care of his mother and forgiving those who were putting him to death. To the very last, he was kind.

Now, one of the best tributes we can pay to Jesus is to take up his torch of kindness—to love as he loved, to care as he cared, to forgive as he forgave, to live as he lived to the very last in the spirit of kindness.

The best tribute we can pay our Lord is to let his kindness live on in us.

9

Why Is Gratitude So Important?

Spiritually speaking, the disposition of ingratitude is as debilitating to our souls as anything I can think of now.

This was part of the prodigal son's problems. He wasn't grateful for what he had; he had no thanksgiving in his heart, no appreciation for his father or brother; and that ungrateful disposition almost ruined him.

We read how later he "came to himself." Isn't that another way of saying he remembered his home and his father, and he rediscovered the spirit of gratitude? Gratitude is important because it reminds us of who we are and whose we are, of our need of God and our need of one another.

The importance of gratitude is underscored in Thomas Gaddis's book *Birdman of Alcatraz*. The book (which was made into a movie starring Burt Lancaster) is the true story of a convicted criminal and two-time murderer, Robert Stroud, who spent most of his seventy years behind bars and in solitary confinement. For the first twenty years of his imprisonment, Robert Stroud was withdrawn, bitter, dangerous, hostile, and hard to handle.

But then something happened to change all that. One day as Stroud was exercising in the prison courtyard, he found a tiny sparrow that had fallen from its nest in a storm. His first impulse was to step on the sparrow and kill it just as he had snuffed out human life. But he didn't. Stroud felt something he hadn't felt for many years: compassion. He tenderly picked up the bird, carried it to his cell, and gently nursed it back to health. His interest was aroused, and he read everything he could on the subject of birds. Other prisoners brought sick birds to him, and he doctored them. He discovered new cures. Before long, Robert Stroud, the dangerous, hardened criminal had become a quiet, serious, respected authority on birds.

His rehabilitation had begun shortly after he had found that first fallen sparrow, as depicted in the movie, when he asked the prison guard (a man to whom previously he had refused to speak) for the orange crate on which the guard sat so that he might make a cage for the sparrow. The guard answered: "Why should I give you this crate, Stroud? For twenty years I've tried to get through to you and be nice to you, but you never gave me the time of day!" But after a few minutes of silence, the guard had a change of heart and slipped the orange crate into Stroud's cell.

When Robert Stroud saw the crate, he looked up at the guard and said something he hadn't said in more than twenty years: "Thank you"!

For the first time in twenty years, Robert Stroud felt gratitude. He was able to say thank you, and that was the moment when his rehabilitation began. He had "come to himself," as did the prodigal son. He realized his indebtedness to others. He realized that he needed help, that he was not the isolated, self-sufficient, independent character he had pretended to be for so long.

In the same way, it is only when you and I can say thank you and mean it that we begin to understand who we are and whose we are. Only when the ugly disposition of ingratitude gives way to the spirit of thankfulness do we begin to capture the spirit of Christ. This was a part of his greatness. Those wonderful attitudes of appreciation that manifest themselves especially with regard to little things—a cup of cold water; the flowers, the grass, a broom, leaven, candles, bread, fish, little children. All of these spoke to him of the goodness of God. That attitude of gratitude is our calling. Anything less, any ingratitude is a virus in our souls that infects everything we do or say or touch.

Ingratitude might seem to be a little thing, but it can devastate your life and the lives of those around you.

What's the Difference Between Childishness and Childlikeness?

I think we need to become more childlike. The pressures of our society tend to make us cold and calculating and image-conscious. Of course we want to be mature, but the quality of childlikeness is part of that maturity, and it's an essential ingredient in happiness, joy, enthusiasm, and Christian discipleship.

We see it in Mark 10. Jesus has come to the region of Judea and great crowds are coming to see him and hear him teach. Jesus gets into heavy discussion with the Pharisees on the weighty matters of divorce and adultery. And then come the children.

The disciples—perhaps caught up with their own self-importance as followers of the great teacher—see the children as a nuisance, an annoyance. So they begin to direct traffic. "Get back there! Get those children out of here! This is serious business! We don't have time for this! We are doing big things here! Don't bother the master! Stand back! Keep quiet!"

When I picture that scene, several images come to mind. For one, the disciples remind me of Barney Fife on the old *Andy Griffith Show.* Barney strutted proudly through the streets of Mayberry, directed traffic, was caught up in his own self-importance, polished his image, took himself too seriously, stuck out his chest, shined his badge, and reminded everyone over and over again that he was the law, that he was the deputy sheriff of Mayberry.

The disciples also remind me of a man who was a member of a church I attended some years ago. This man was an usher and a good one until the church sent him to Indiana, paid his way to a weeklong ushers' school, and lived to regret it.

When he returned, he was so "over-trained" that his ushering took on gigantic proportions; he was the "main event" of the worship service. He directed the people as if he were a combination of an enthusiastic traffic cop, Leonard Bernstein conducting the New York Philharmonic, and a circus ringmaster. He gave so much effort and made so much noise shushing the children and youth that they soon referred to him as the "Head Shusher."

And the disciples remind me of a pep squad sponsor for a peewee football team I saw recently. The woman, in her early forties, and her pep squad sat prim and proper with uniforms and white gloves doing their cheers systematically. I was sitting just behind them.

All went well until their team scored a touchdown and the pep squad came unglued, jumping up and down and cheering. This infuriated the sponsor. Red-faced, she screamed for them to sit down and straighten up their rows and be more systematic in their cheering.

She said, "I'm ashamed of all of you. When I was your age, I was in a pep squad and I never acted like that!" Then one of the little pep squad girls sitting right in front of me muttered out loud, "She was never our age!"

Of course, she was their age at one time, but somehow over the years, the quality of childlikeness had gotten lost. You could see the problem written in the worried look on her face.

The disciples likewise rebuked the children, and when Jesus saw it, he was displeased. He was indignant and he said, "Allow the children to come to me. Don't forbid them, because God's kingdom belongs to people like these children" (Luke 18:16).

Jesus' call here is of course not to childishness, but to childlikeness. He probably is referring to the qualities of genuineness, receptivity, dependence, trust, openness, affection, curiosity, energy, and enthusiasm. These are all characteristics of children and they are characteristic of the Christian life and discipleship.

Elton Trueblood, a noted theologian and professor of the twentieth century, said it well: "We tend to glorify adulthood and wisdom and worldly prudence, but the gospel reverses all this. The gospel says that the inescapable condition of entrance into the divine fellowship is that we turn and become as a little child...tender and full of wonder and unspoiled by the hard skepticism on which we so often pride ourselves." Andrew Gillies said it poetically:

> Last night my little boy confessed to me
> Some childish wrong;
> And kneeling at my knee,
> He prayed with tears—
> "Dear God, make me a man
> Like Daddy—wise and strong;
> I know you can."
> Then, while he slept
> I knelt beside his bed,
> Confessed my sins,
> And prayed with low-bowed head—
> O God, make me a child
> Like my child here—
> Pure, guileless
> Trusting Thee with faith sincere.

Do You Build Walls or Bridges?

Some years ago, I saw some young people present a special play one Sunday evening. The play was called *Construction*. The production opened with a group of people gathered in an otherworldly kind of place. They don't know where they are, or how they got there, or what they are supposed to do.

They discuss this: Where are we? Why are we in this place? What is our purpose here? What are we supposed to do? Who put us here?

At this point, they notice that there are some building materials there, so they decide that they obviously are supposed to build something. But what? Someone in the group wants to build a swimming pool. Another wants to build a hospital or an infirmary.

But then someone in the group says something like: "We are not alone here. I have been hearing the noises of other people. We don't know who they are or what these others are like or what they are up to, and we can't afford to take a chance. It's too risky. We need to get a wall up before it's too late."

As they discuss this further, they become frightened and decide that this person is right. They should build a wall to protect themselves from those people out there. So they organize and begin to build a formidable wall. After they have worked for some time on their wall, they look up one day to see someone coming their way. When the stranger arrives, he tells them that he is a builder and that the one who put them there sent him to help them—and that he has the blueprints that will show them what they are supposed to build.

Then he tells them that they are not supposed to build a wall. Rather, they are supposed to build a bridge to bring people together, not a wall to shut them out. Upon hearing this, the members of the group are enraged. They become angry with the builder—and suspicious. Who is this man? Who does he think he is, disrupting our plans like this? After all, our wall is almost finished.

"Wait a minute," they say. "Maybe he is a spy. Maybe he is trying to trap us." In a frenzied panic, they decide that the builder is a troublemaker and that they must get rid of this troublemaker with the blueprints. They all charge and attack him.

At this point in the play, the lights go out, the organ music swells and rumbles loudly, and the group shouts hostilities. Next come complete silence and darkness. Then a single spotlight comes on to reveal that the young builder who wanted them to build a bridge rather than a wall has been crucified.

The play ends as the group shrinks back in horror at what they have done. Then, quietly and shamefully, one of the characters says, "We have to learn; we just have to learn. We can't go on crucifying the TRUTH forever!"

Now this to me is a very powerful play. It's an unusual but relevant play for us right now because all around us people are still building walls: walls constructed of fear and pride and anxiety, walls made of prejudice and closed minds, walls that separate people and spread suspicion, walls that fence us in and shut others out.

But the good news of the play is that Jesus Christ is the young builder with the blueprints, and his truth can't be killed. It won't die; it resurrects. The truth is that he wants us to tear down our walls. The truth is that he wants us to be bridge builders.

1 2

Have You Ever Experienced God's Surprising, Reconciling Presence?

There is nothing more beautiful than the picture of recon-ciliation, especially when it comes as a surprise! To see people who have been bitterly separated, cut off, or estranged suddenly back together in love and harmony is a moving and inspiring experience.

I saw this happen in a most unlikely place: an administra-tive board meeting in a little United Methodist church in the Midwest. I was pastor of that church, and I had dreaded that meeting more than words can express. We were going to have a knock-down, drag-out meeting that night, and I knew it was coming. I had been forewarned. A certain man had hurt feelings, and he was coming to disrupt the meeting.

He was mad at another man, and he was going to unleash his anger at the board meeting that Wednesday night. We had just completed a new education building. We were making plans to open and dedicate it. But this man was determined to stop us!

Why? His feelings were hurt. He had been on every building project committee at the church for thirty years, but somehow he was left off this committee for this project. He was hurt and angry. He felt unneeded and left out and for months, while the education building was going up, he had been seething.

He was especially upset with the chairman of the building committee. He was convinced that everything was done wrong and that the building was hazardous and unsafe for our children. He had personally inspected the building and was coming to the board meeting to block the opening of the educational wing. He had a long list of grievances. He had a long list of glaring errors made by the committee. He had an even longer list of things that the building committee chairman had done that were wrong, unsafe, and illegal.

He was upset and he took it out on the board that night. It was terrible.

He attacked the chairman. The chairman fought back. Voices were raised. People began to choose sides. Tension hung heavy in the room. Jealousy, envy, resentment, and pettiness fueled the night.

The board chairman, flustered by the whole thing, tried to resolve it by calling for a vote. He said, "Everyone for [that man's] side raise your hand." But then came a woman's voice from the back of the room: "Wait a minute, Mr. Chairman.

Before we vote on anything, I want to say something." With tears glistening in her eyes, she began to speak. My, how she spoke!

"What is all this talk about sides? What is all this talk about this one's side and that one's side? We are a church! We don't choose sides. We are all on the same side. We are all on God's side. We are a family here. We're God's family. Sides? It breaks my heart to hear us squabble like this. It must break God's heart, too!"

With that, she sat down. There was not a sound in that room. In the silence we realized that she was right. We were all ashamed of how we had been acting.

Then the unhappy man stood up. Nervously, he cleared his throat and softly said, "I'm so sorry. And I want to apologize to all of you, but especially to [the building committee chairman]. I don't know what got into me. Maybe I was jealous. Maybe I felt left out. But I know now that I was wrong, and I'm sorry."

Then he walked over to the building committee chairman, extended his hand, and quietly said, "Can you ever forgive me?"

The chairman stood, shook the man's hand, and then, smiling through his tears, gave him a big bear hug. And all the board members stood and applauded. And then they all began hugging one another!

I thought to myself, "How beautiful is the picture of reconciliation!" And under my breath I muttered with a sigh of relief some words from the Book of Genesis: "The LORD is definitely in this place, but I didn't know it" (28:16).

1 3

Are You Talking More
and Communicating Less?

A re we talking more and communicating less? Many people feel that this is the wordiest period in human history.
We seem to be literally bombarded by words. Everywhere we
go, people are chattering.

We turn on the radio and are assaulted by the loud, inces-
sant voice of a disc jockey. We turn on the television and
someone is telling us about a product that we cannot live
without. We buy music by our favorite recording artist only
to discover that he decided to talk on this one instead of sing.

In his book *Religion Without Wrappings*, David H. C.
Read said that when he was a prisoner of war, the people in
the concentration camp learned a true economy of speech.
Living daily with death and deprivation, they became
strangely silent. The prisoners, perhaps in fear of calling too
much attention to themselves, spoke only when it was necessary. When the war ended and they were released to return

home, their most memorable impression of their homecomings was that everyone was talking, talking, talking.

And yet despite the bombardment of words, despite the amazing advances in the technology of communication, the truth is that we are talking more and communicating less. There are more lonely, isolated people in our world today than ever before—people who feel unaccepted, unheard, and cut off.

Centenary College sponsored a telephone emergency listening service called Open Ear. A person with a problem or a need to talk could call Open Ear and find a helpful, sympathetic listener. A friend of mine who worked with Open Ear told me that the calls were almost invariably from people who felt that they are all alone in the world and had no one to talk with. With all the people and with all the attempts at communication they still felt lonely, estranged, cut off, and isolated.

How strange it is that we live in a time of open communication, and yet fail so terribly to bridge the gap between persons. The technological advances in communication have been incredible. George Washington said of his ambassador to France: "We haven't heard from Ben Franklin in Paris this year. We should write him a letter." Now, we measure the time required for communication around the globe not merely in seconds, but in nanoseconds. Despite all this, it still may be true that we are talking more and communicating less!

Communication means more than giving out information. It means sharing life together. And it happens only when persons reach out in openness to one another to touch and share and care. It happens only when they truly and deeply know one another as God-created persons. It is significant to note that the words *communion* and *communication* come from the same root word. They have to do with coming together, sharing, and becoming united.

In the beginning of John's Gospel, Christ is called "the Word." "The Word became flesh and made his home among us" (John 1:14). What does that mean? Perhaps it's that in Jesus of Nazareth we see the truth of God, the idea of God communicated, wrapped up in a person. In him, we see life as God meant it.

As Helen Kromer puts it in a dramatic reading called "The Word," we communicate with one another using words. We hardly even think about it. But, as she says:

> Speak to my very small son and the words mean nothing, for he does not know my language. And so I must show him: "This is your foot, and it is meant for walking."...And one day "walking" shapes in his brain with the word. God had something to say to Man, but the words meant nothing, for we did not know his language. And so we were shown: "Behold the man!...This is...Man as I mean him, loving and serving. I have put him in flesh. Now the word has shape and form and substance to travel between us. Let him show forth love till one day 'loving' shapes in your brain with the Word."

The key to communication is love. When loving shapes in our brains, then we can become good communicators.

Do You Love Anyone Like That?

More than any other thing, Jesus came to teach us how to love unconditionally. In Jesus we see what God is like. In him, God is saying, "This is how I love all of you. My love for you is unconditional. Nothing you can do will stop me from loving you. You can betray me, you can deny me, you can taunt me, you can beat me, you can curse me, you can spit on me, you can nail me to a cross…and I will keep on loving you. There is nothing in all the world that you can do to me that will stop me from loving. I love you like that—unconditionally!"

And that is the way God wants us to love one another. I can't say "I will love you if you are good" or "I will love you if you are nice to me" or "I will love you if you will love me back." I can't say that and live in the spirit of Christ. The only way I can live in his spirit is to love unconditionally, to love expecting nothing in return, to love unselfishly.

There is an interesting legend that comes out of ancient Greece that shows the danger of putting conditions on our love for others. According to the legend, two Greek athletes were close friends, like brothers. But then one began to get more recognition—so much so that the townspeople built a statue honoring him as their top athlete.

The other man became insanely jealous—so much so that every night after dark he would go out and try to destroy the statue. Finally he succeeded. He toppled the heavy statue off its pedestal, but it fell on him and crushed him to death. He was destroyed by his own jealousy, crushed by his own envy.

Unconditional love is the opposite of that.

Robert E. Lee was once asked his opinion of a certain man. General Lee responded: "He is a fine and able man and I commend him to you highly!"

"But, General," the questioner protested, "don't you know how this man talks behind your back? Don't you know the terrible things he says about you?"

"Yes," Lee answered, "I know, but you didn't ask how he felt about me. You asked me what I think of him…and I think he is a fine and able man and I commend him to you highly."

That is unconditional love and it is our calling as Christian disciples. Unconditional love: we see it dramatically in Jesus' parable of the prodigal son. The parable is not well named because it is about a father and two sons, and the father—not the son—is the hero. In the father, we see the central truth Jesus wanted to communicate through the story: unconditional love! Love with no strings attached!

The prodigal rejects his father and runs away to the far country and squanders away his money in riotous living. But then he comes to his senses and returns home, penitent and humble. He rehearses his confession all the way. When he comes face-to-face with his father, the prodigal begins to blurt out his confession. But the father interrupts him. He doesn't want to hear it. He wants to get on with the celebration. Forgiveness and love were there all along.

The prodigal had only to come back and accept them. No talk needed, no excuses necessary, no "I told you so's" expressed, no "pound of flesh" demanded, just love freely given. The father runs with joy to greet and receive the prodigal and then calls for a celebration. "Bring out the best robe and put it on him! Put a ring on his finger and sandals on his feet! Fetch the fattened calf and slaughter it. We must celebrate with feasting because this son of mine was dead and has come back to life! He was lost and is found" (Luke 15:22-24).

That is the picture of unconditional love. More than that, it is the picture of how Jesus saw God, how Jesus understood God to be: a gracious, merciful, compassionate father; not a vindictive judge, but a tender, loving, caring father.

That is good news: God loves us unconditionally. It is also a challenge because that's the way he wants us to love one another.

Do you love anyone like that? Do you love anyone unconditionally?

That's something to think about, isn't it?

1 5

Did Jesus Really Mean That?

A few years ago, I was on the campus of a small college during their Religious Emphasis Week. The theme of the week was "The Hard Sayings of Jesus." One evening in one of the dormitories, I was leading a discussion on some of these difficult teachings such as "turn the other cheek," "love your enemies," and "go the second mile."

One young man said, "The teachings of Jesus are difficult for me because I'm not sure I understand them."

Another student said, "I see it just the other way around. They are difficult for me because I think I do understand them, but I'm not so sure I want to do them!"

When you study the Gospels closely, you come face-to-face with the frustrating fact that Jesus said some very perplexing things. These "difficult sayings" have puzzled many devout Bible readers over the years. In addition, critics of Christianity have seen in these mysterious passages an opportunity for discounting the truth and the relevance of what Jesus taught. Even during his ministry, what Jesus said was often misunderstood by his hearers, even by his own disciples.

A valid example of this is found in John 6:60, where some of the disciples exclaim: "This message is harsh. Who can hear it?" The New English Bible makes it even more dramatic by translating it: "This is more than we can stomach! Why listen to such words?" Then, a few verses later, we find this haunting verse: "From that time on, many of his disciples withdrew and no longer went about with him" (v. 66 NEB).

The difficulty is not just in understanding what Jesus meant. In a real sense we could say that when we understand the difficult sayings of Jesus, our difficulty has just begun! We run head-on into the startling challenges of living the Christian faith.

As Jesus saw it, being a Christian disciple meant living in a special kind of sacrificial, self-giving spirit. You may call it magnanimity, generosity, bigness, graciousness, selflessness, or unconditional love. Whatever label you put on it, Jesus is saying, "Live in this spirit!" That's where the real difficulty begins.

He is saying respond to harshness with kindness; respond to cruelty with tenderness; respond to hurt with forgiveness; respond to adversity with perseverance; respond to hate with love.

Can Jesus really mean this? The world scoffs at this and, with the disciples in John's Gospel, says, "Wait a minute now. This is more than we can stomach. How can we listen to this? There must be some mistake here. Life doesn't work that way!"

But Jesus is saying that this is precisely the way life does work. "A sensitive answer turns back wrath" (Proverbs 15:1). Love is indeed the most powerful thing in the world! The only way you and I can be authentic disciples of Christ is to believe this and stake our lives on it and give our lives to it.

To live in this gracious spirit is the calling of every Christian. It is the main message of the Sermon on the Mount. The real difficulty is not so much in understanding what Jesus meant. The real difficulty comes when we do understand what he meant, when we do understand that he meant what he said. He meant it so much that he saw such qualities as the most authentic marks of discipleship. He meant it so much that he gave his life for it. The real difficulty is in believing what he said enough to try it.

Won't you try it? Try it diligently for one day, and it will change your life forever.

When God Speaks, Can the Church Be Our Hearing Aid?

Teenagers today are not content with the factory-made sound systems that come in most cars. Instead they prefer to install additional systems in their cars, then add numerous speakers in strategic locations to distribute the sound. Next, they add a power booster to make the sound louder, and on and on.

All of this is done to enhance the sound and to enable them to hear their music better. Now this is all well and good for them because they understand the system; they know how to operate it, they know what to expect, and they like the music loud. But if an innocent, naive, unsuspecting adult happens to get in the car and push the power booster button, he is likely in for the shock of his life! The sound will hit him in the face so forcefully that his ears will be pinned back against his head, his hair will stand straight up on end, and he will be a prime candidate for whiplash! In a sense, the power booster could be called a modern-day version of a hearing aid.

All the way from the cumbersome primitive ear trumpet to more attractive—even invisible—devices, hearing aids have been wonderfully helpful to those who need them.

In a way, this is precisely what the church does for us. The church is our hearing aid today. God speaks, but we need assistance in hearing the message clearly. The church can help us to tune in.

For example, God speaks a word of calling, and the church is our hearing aid. God calls us to service, to mission, to ministry. The church (when it is at its best) helps us to hear God's call and to respond. The church teaches us that God chooses to use us, that he chooses to work through us. "I've got a job for you!" That is God's calling to each of us. "I want to put you to work!" "You are important to me!" "You are valuable to me!" "There is a special job that only you can do!"

That is God's word to us, a word of calling and sometimes our natural ears just can't take it in. That's where the church comes in as our hearing aid.

Or God speaks a word of love, and the church is our hearing aid. Let me ask you something. What was the very first verse of Scripture you learned as a child in Sunday school? Mine was "God is love" (1 John 4:8).

Do you remember the first song you learned as a child in Sunday school? Mine was "Jesus Loves Me!" The second was "Praise Him, All Ye Little Children."

That's the good news of our faith. The message of God's love is the message the church most wants us to hear.

Or God speaks a word of forgiveness, and the church is our hearing aid. The church teaches us that God is forgiving and wants us to be forgiving. This is the point of the parable of the prodigal son. We see one who needs forgiveness, one who gives forgiveness, and one who is unwilling to forgive. This great parable of the church clearly shows that the father's willingness to forgive was right and that the elder brother's unwillingness to forgive was wrong—and that it kept him out of the celebration. The church reminds us over and over of God's forgiving ways and how he wants us to be forgiving in the same way.

God is speaking. The church, like a hearing aid, can help us hear.

Do You Know Firsthand the Grace of God that Sets Us Free?

When I was in seminary, I had a classmate who was a real character! If I had to make a list of the most unusual characters I have ever met, he easily would be in the top ten.

He always wore a black suit, a white shirt, and a solid black tie...and he always carried a large black umbrella. He was of German descent and proud of it. Sometimes he would speak to me in German, sometimes in Ohio English, and sometimes he would try to speak in a southern drawl. He was not making fun; he thought it made me more comfortable.

He was a rare and wonderful character. He was the talk of the seminary, not for his eccentric ways, however, but because in our first year of theological school, he hadn't worked out his theology yet. And he had (like Martin Luther, whom he so much admired) a troubled soul.

This guy, like Luther in his early years, had a bad image of God. Like Luther, he was scared to death of God, and this fear was reflected most graphically in his attitude toward the altar. The altar table in the seminary chapel was quite simple, actually, just a white table with a cross and two candles on it. But it struck fear in my classmate's heart because it represented for him the presence of God, and he was scared of God.

We had chapel every day, and every day the students would rush to chapel to see how he would "handle the altar today."

- On some days, he would stand in the back of the chapel with his head bowed, and he would pray silently.
- On some days, he would walk all the way up to the altar and kneel before it.
- Or he might fall down on all fours before it.
- On some days, he would stand and look at the altar in deep meditation.
- On other days he would make the sign of the cross.
- And when we had Communion, he would always slip up to the altar after the service and eat all the leftover bread and drink all the leftover grape juice—because they had been consecrated, and he felt that to consecrate the elements and then not eat all of them would somehow make God angry.

Once, in preaching class, he accidentally walked between the altar and the congregation. Horrified, he grabbed his head, turned, and did a deep bow. Then he rushed to the pulpit, stammered out an apology and, unable to preach, ran out of the chapel with tears in his eyes.

He was frustrated, ill-at-ease, and confused. Later he admitted that his confusion came from his fear of God.

Everything he did, he did to try to win God's love, to appease God, to get God to forgive him and accept him. He felt that God was angry with him until one day when he wrote a paper on Jesus' parable of the prodigal son. As he studied those words of Jesus that make up what some have called the greatest short story in the world, he discovered something that set him free. He discovered through the mind of Jesus and the words of Jesus that he didn't have to win God's love. He already had it. God had loved him all along!

In that parable, Jesus painted God's picture, and he painted God boldly and tenderly as a *loving father*—not as an austere, impersonal, hostile God who is out to get us. He painted God as a loving father who runs down the road to meet us, who celebrates our homecoming because he cares for us, because he has good will for us.

My classmate discovered through studying the Scriptures that God loves us, that God is on our side, that God is a caring father. That is good news, isn't it?

Is Jesus God's Way of Getting Rid of a Bad Reputation?

There's a story about a little boy who was afraid of the dark, and he kept calling out to his mother. Trying to console him, his mother said to him, "You don't have to be afraid. God is there with you."

"I know that," answered the little boy, "but I want someone in here with me that's got a face."

Well, that is the point. Jesus gives God a face. And the good news is that it's the face of love, concern, acceptance, and compassion. The key characteristic of the life and message of Jesus is that it is a gospel. The word *gospel* (*euangel ion* in Greek) means good news. Not bad news.

It was good news that Jesus came to bring. If Jesus came to bring good news about God, then it must mean that he came to tell people things about God that they did not know or did not realize before! Before Jesus, people thought of God as unapproachable and unpredictable, distant and detached, holy and hidden, unfeeling and indifferent.

In fact, the oldest and most primitive idea about God was that God was hostile and grudging toward people. The gods begrudged people everything they attained, achieved, or received. To be successful, prosperous, or great was dangerous; mediocrity alone was safe.

Herodotus found a corollary in the fact that the tallest trees were most likely to be blasted by the lightning strike; just so, any man who did too well or achieved too much was in danger of being blasted by the gods. The classic story that illustrates this primitive notion of the hostile god is that of Prometheus.

Prometheus cared for people. He therefore stole fire from heaven, gave it to people, and taught them how to use it. This angered Zeus, the chief of gods, so much that he caused Prometheus to be chained to a rock in Scythia. Then he sent an eagle to tear out Prometheus's liver every day. Prometheus's liver would grow back nightly because of his immortality, only to be torn out again, until finally Hercules came to set him free.

The story graphically illustrates the point of humans fearing gods. Before Jesus, people were afraid of God. Before Jesus, people thought God was hostile toward them. Before Jesus, people thought they were the victims of God, rather than the children of God. These primitive notions, of course, led to the idea of offering a sacrificial lamb on the altar to appease God's wrath or to win God's approval. But then came Jesus with his picture of God as a gracious, merciful, loving father.

With this in mind, we can better understand John Killinger's classic quote: "Jesus is God's way of getting rid of a bad reputation!"

Anybody Here Enjoy
Religion?

Some years ago, a train stopped somewhere in southern Georgia to take on water for the engine. A man on the train saw an old-timer leaning against the depot platform and yelled to him, "Anybody around here enjoy religion?" The old-timer on the platform shuffled his feet and then replied, "Them that has does!"

Now, wouldn't you like to find that old fellow and shake his hand? He accomplished much with his answer. He spoke four words and made four grammatical errors! It should be noted that although his grammar was terrible, his theology was terrific. Forget how he said it, and remember what he said: "Them that has does!"

That translates: "Those who really have religion are radiantly joyous people!" Real religion does not make us somber, sullen, and sad; rather, real faith makes us happy, confident, and glad.

Unfortunately, a great host of people (and this includes many in the churches) have not made this discovery. They do not think of religion as a source of joy. They are pious, but not happy. They are conscientious, but not radiant. They are dedicated, but not joyful. Their personalities are for the most part grim, serious, heavy, burdened. They scowl more than they smile.

There's a story about the little boy who went to church one Sunday morning with his grandmother, whose approach to religion was stern and puritanical. The little boy saw a friend and smiled at him. The grandmother slapped his hand and said in a stage whisper: "Quit that grinning! Don't smile like that in church."

How sad it is—indeed, how tragic—that some people see religion as a source of goodness, but not as a source of gladness. How sad that some people see religion as a sensitizer of conscience, but not as a fountain of happiness.

A spoonerism is an accidental transposition of sounds, usually the initial sounds of two or more words. For example, you mean to say a "well-oiled bicycle" and it comes out a "well-boiled icicle." That is a spoonerism. This kind of verbal blooper is named for the Reverend William A. Spooner, who was a professor at New College, Oxford, some years ago. He was famous for such mistakes.

One of the most noted of all the verbal mistakes attributed to Spooner was this one. He meant to say, "The cheerful tidings of the gospel," but it came out, "The tearful chidings of the gospel."

In that spoonerism—in capsule form—is one of the saddest mistakes in the history of religion; namely the fact that some well-meaning religious people have forgotten that our Christian faith is good news of great joy. They have lost touch with the "cheerful tidings of the gospel" and have chosen instead to come down hard, heavy, and threatening with the "tearful chidings."

This is, of course, a great pity because our world desperately needs Christian people who are radiant and happy, joyful and confident—people who, as Paul put it, rejoice always!

If there is one thing the Christian gospel offers us, it is joy—not a silly giddiness, but a deep abiding joy that stays with us even in the darkest circumstances. Happiness, gladness, abundant living are certainly a part of Christ's legacy to us, his people:

"I have said these things to you so that my joy will be in you and your joy will be complete" (John 15:11).

Do You Make Excuses, Excuses, Excuses?

At one point in the monumental historical novel by Tolstoy, *War and Peace*, the lead character, Pierre, is forced to face himself and make an honest analysis of his life. He says it for all of us, "Yes, I have sinned, but I have several excellent excuses!" Don't we all? We have several excellent excuses for just about everything we have done or might want to do. Whatever the situation, there is an ever-ready excuse available.

Take the matter of missing church. Over the years, I have heard some great excuses for failure to make it to church. Some blame the weather, others company, still others clothing. One woman in a church I served fascinated me with her excuse. In the five years I was pastor there, she never made it to church. It seemed that I was always running into her in crowded basketball arenas, theaters, or parties, and she would always say, "Oh, Jim, I do wish I could come to church, but I can't stand to be in a crowd." I'm still trying to figure that one out!

However, my favorite was given to me buy a woman who said, "I don't go to church and this is my reason: if I go some of the time, it makes me want to go all the time. So I don't go any of the time, and this keeps me from feeling guilty and wanting to go all of the time."

What about unfaithfulness? This is the most amazingly excused sin in the world. It has even been called (of all things) the "new morality." We call it the "new morality" and dupe ourselves because it is the oldest idolatry in the world.

Take the matter of gossip. It is dangerous, cruel, hurtful, devastating, and sinful; yet we indulge in it so frequently and excuse it so lightly. I once heard a woman excuse her gossip by saying, "I won't tell anything about another person unless it is good, and boy is this good!"

Then there is temper. Have you ever heard someone say something like this: "Oh, everybody knows I was born with a hot temper, but my temper is like a cyclone. It blows up quickly and just as quickly blows away." What people with bad tempers don't realize is that their tempers, also like cyclones, leave behind immeasurable hurt, agony, heartache, and devastation.

Yes, we have sinned, but we have several excellent excuses! We are living in very frank times when nothing is kept under wraps. People will admit to almost anything. So our problem is not that we hesitate to admit anything, but rather that we are learning how to justify everything.

Now, what about these excuses? What does the Christian faith say to us about our excuse-making?

God sees through our excuses. Like a father who knows his children well, God knows us—better than we know ourselves. God can't be conned. Our excuses seem so frail and feeble when laid up under the light of God's truth.

God is not so much interested in hearing our excuses as forgiving our sins. We don't need a scapegoat; we have a savior. Christ came to show us that forgiveness is at hand. When the prodigal son comes home and begins to blurt his well-worded confession, the father interrupts him. He doesn't want to hear it. He wants to get on with the celebration. The point is clear. We are not justified by our eloquent excuses, but by the grace of a loving, forgiving father.

What God wants is not excuses, but penitence. What is said with the lips is not nearly so important as what happens in the heart. The Pharisee and Publican went to the temple to pray. The Pharisee tried to excuse himself with high-sounding words. But there was the Publican with his prayer of penitence, "God, be merciful to me, a sinner!" As the parable closes, the penitent Publican is justified, rather than the excuse-making Pharisee.

What God wants is not excuses, but penitence, commitment, and acts of love.

2 1

Are You Standing in the Need of Prayer?

The truth is that if we don't pray, our relationship with God will fade and our faith will shrink.

It's like an experience I had with a childhood friend. We went through school together—grammar school, junior high, and high school. We were real buddies. We walked to school together, we played ball together, we worked together. Once we even studied together! We did everything together.

We were close. We knew each other so well that sometimes we knew what was going on in each other's minds. But then we graduated. He went to work, and I went away to college. The four years of college passed, and then I went farther away to seminary.

We lost contact. There was no communication between us. Some years later we met, and we discovered that we were not the same; the relationship was not the same. We were like strangers to each other. We had trouble having a conversation. We didn't really feel comfortable with each other. We no longer felt close to each other because we had lost each other, because we had lost contact. Once we had been so close. Now we were strangers because we had not been communicating. This same kind of thing can happen in our relationship with God. If we do not pray, we find our relationship with God growing dimmer and weaker.

One of our problems with prayer, I think, is that we mistakenly think that prayer requires a special kind of holy-sounding language that boasts of pious phrases and pontifical tones. That's not true. Prayer is conversation with God. We don't have to have a special language or sanctimonious tone. All we have to have is a willingness to communicate and talk to God.

If we can come to prayer remembering that God is our friend, it helps. A friend is one with whom we can share our joys and sorrows, our victories and defeats, our confidences and our worries, our deepest thoughts and lightest wonderings.

A minister tells of teaching a man how to pray. The man came to this minister's office and said, "I cannot pray. I want to talk to God, but I just can't do it. I don't know how."

The minister asked him, "If you could pray, what would you want to say to God?"

The man thought for a moment, and then he shared some beautiful thoughts and ideas. When he finished, the minister got up and said, "What I want you to do is to look at that chair and, if you can, imagine God sitting there instead of me. After I go, I want you to try to say to the chair and the image of God, everything you told me. Just tell it like you told it to me."

With that, the minister left the office. A few moments later, the man came out. His face was beaming as he said, "I was able to do it. I began to talk to that chair...and then I began to imagine God was sitting there. I felt his presence. I found myself saying a lot of things I never thought I could say. It wasn't as hard as I thought. It was good."

We can do that, can't we? In fact, we need to do it to keep our faith alive. If we don't pray, if we don't communicate with God, our faith will shrink and shrivel and weaken.

What Shall I Do to Inherit Eternal Life?

In a sense, the rich young ruler's problem was that he wanted a simple solution. When he came to Jesus in search of real life—in search of something to fill the inner emptiness gnawing in him, in search of something to satisfy that deep hunger in his soul—he wanted no complicated personal involvement. He wanted an easy answer, an instant miracle, a simple solution.

But when Jesus told him that this was no simple matter, that this is a life commitment and touches all that you have and all that you are, the rich young man turned away sorrowfully. He wanted a quick, easy, simple remedy.

In the story Jesus has set his face toward Jerusalem. He is on his way to the holy city, on his way to the cross. This is serious business now. He is thinking deep thoughts when the rich young ruler runs up and kneels before him and asks about life. There are some fascinating things to notice here.

This man is a *rich young ruler.* He has all the things we so openly long for: wealth, youth, power. Some would say, "He has it made! He has it all! Wealth, youth, power—what more could he want?" But something is missing in his life. He knows it, feels it, senses it. Something is missing! There is a void, an emptiness, a hunger that is not satisfied, a thirst that is not quenched. Money, power, youthfulness are not enough! Something more is needed to make his life full. He knows that his life is incomplete, so he comes to Jesus in search of a simple solution. After all, he probably is used to getting exactly what he wants, simply and quickly. He is a ruler. When he speaks, people say, "Yes, sir." When he calls, people jump and come immediately. When he wants something, people step up and fetch it.

Now, although we are not rich young rulers, that mind-set is not alien to us. In a sense, we have become a spoiled people who are impatient with delays, detours, or even disciplines. We want things done for us quickly and simply. Why wait or work for anything? We are bombarded by fast-service advertisements every day: "Pay $1 down, get it now." "Clothes cleaned—one hour." "Cars washed—two minutes."

We itch for the instantaneous: instant coffee, instant biscuits, instant cereal. We are impatient people who look for near ways, shortcuts, quick results, simple solutions. And usually we want somebody else to do it all for us.

But we must beware of oversimplification. The things that matter most in life do not come quickly, easily, or simply. We often forget this. Like the rich young ruler, we get in a hurry and want instant answers and easy one-two-three solutions. We forget that "God's mills grind slow but sure."

When we get too easily and reach too quickly, we tend to appreciate too lightly! The things that matter most in life take time, effort, sacrifice, thought, commitment, and hard work. To be sure, some things you can get immediately by pushing buttons or paying money down. But the great things, the real values, do not come that way. They have to be grown and cultivated. You can get a sports car or a speedboat with a quick down payment. But character, faith, morality, maturity, spiritual strength: you have to commit your whole life to these things and grow them slowly, but surely.

Do You Really Know the Good News?

L ook at the "positive don'ts" of Jesus. The "positive don'ts" is a strange-sounding phrase because we usually think of the words *positive* and *don't* as contradictory terms, or as opposites. The word *don't* has a negative tone for us, not a positive one. In fact, some people are actually turned off by religion because of the numerous, prohibitive, and legalistic "don'ts" they hear.

One day in a service station, a young man in his late twenties asked me about our church. We visited for a moment and then I invited him to visit our church. "Oh no, not yet," he answered. "I'm having too much fun sowing my wild oats. To tell you the truth," he continued, "I'm really hoping for one of those neat deathbed conversions!" It's sad that many people mistakenly see the church in such a negative way.

I heard a story about a missionary who years ago was trying to convert a native chief of a primitive tribe. Now the chief was very old, and the missionary was very "Old Testament"; that is, his version of Christianity leaned heavily on the "don'ts" and the "thou shalt nots!" And when he explained the faith, he always seemed to bear down hard on what you can't do, what you mustn't do, what you don't do if you are a Christian, completely ignoring the "good news" and positive principles of faith. The elderly chief listened patiently as the missionary pronounced the negatives in staccato fashion: "Don't do this! Don't do that! Don't do the other!"

Finally, the chief said, "I do not understand this religion of yours. Let me get this straight. You mean I cannot steal?" "That's right," said the missionary. "You mean I cannot take another man's ivory or oxen?" "Quite right," said the missionary. "You mean I cannot dance the war dance or ambush the enemy?" "Quite right!" "You mean I cannot chase after women and get drunk and party all night?" "Absolutely right," said the missionary. "But I can't do any of those things anyway," said the native chief regretfully. "I am too old!" Then he paused and said, "Ah, now I understand. To be old and to be Christian, they are the same thing!"

Now, this is a humorous story and yet really it's not so funny. There are many people around today who share the chief's confusion and misunderstanding of Christianity. They think of God as one who frowns on our fun, slaps our hands, and says continually, "Don't do this! Don't do that! Naughty, naughty, mustn't do!" They think of Christianity as something old, joyless, negative, and prohibitive. For these people, religion is not freeing; it is restrictive. For these people, religion does not give life; it takes life away. This is a terrible, tragic misunderstanding of the Christian faith. The Christian faith is not bad news; it is not simply a list of "don'ts." No, it is positive good news, and that's what Jesus came to show us.

Even the "don'ts" of Jesus have a positive good news ring to them. For example, "Don't be afraid!" That is a positive. It means we shouldn't use our energy worrying ourselves silly over things that do not matter. We just give our energies to loving, serving, and trusting God to bring it all out right. "Don't hate!" This is also positive. It means that we can forgive. We don't have to be resentful or envious or jealous or arrogant. Jesus knew that hating others is not only harmful to them, but it can destroy our own souls. Hate is a spiritual cancer. Jesus knew that and set us free from it. "Don't wait for heaven!" What could be more positive? Heaven can begin for you now and continue beyond the grave. Jesus said, "The kingdom is at hand"; "the kingdom is within you"; "I go to prepare a place for you." I believe in heaven after this life, but we don't have to wait. Heaven can begin now.

Every time real love is expressed, there is heaven. Every time kindness is given, there is heaven. Every time truth prevails and honesty wins and acceptance is felt, there is heaven.

The positive good news of our faith is that God loves us and is with us on both sides of the grave.

What Are the Most Authentic Qualities of Life?

The Roman centurion saw it; he saw the truth as he stood at the foot of the cross. Jesus had just breathed his last, and as the Roman centurion looked up at the Nazarene, his mind darted back over the dramatic crescendo of events that had happened so quickly over the last few hours and days.

- He had seen Jesus riding into Jerusalem on a donkey with palm branches waved before him, recognized as a king and yet not interested in earthly kingdoms.
- He had heard Jesus teaching with keen insight and authority in public places.
- He had seen Jesus arrested, falsely accused and convicted, mocked, jeered, slapped, spat upon.

- He had seen Jesus brutally crucified…and noticed that he never struggled; he never said a "mumblin' word."
- He had heard Jesus pray a prayer for forgiveness in behalf of his executioners.
- He had seen Jesus console the thief on the adjacent cross.
- He had seen Jesus make provisions for the care of his mother even as he was in anguish on a cross.
- And now, the Roman centurion had seen Jesus of Nazareth die, and as he looked up at Jesus hanging there, the centurion said it for all of us: "This man was certainly God's Son" (Mark 15:39).

Could it be that this was the centurion's way of saying that this man was so good, so authentic, so genuine, he must be *true*? He was God's man, God's son, God's word become flesh. God's idea lived out. He was *true* to what God meant life to be.

Even at the place of death, Jesus shows us how to live. Even as he dies, he reveals the most authentic qualities of life. A few of these qualities emerge so graphically from the cross that they must be true, they must be of God.

First is love. Love is so good, so beautiful, so fulfilling, so right that it must be true. Jesus believed that. He went to the cross for it.

Recently, I saw our daughter do something nice and thoughtful for her brother. That simple act of kindness made me feel great joy, and I thought to myself: "There is nothing that makes me happier than to see my children loving each other, helping each other, caring for each other." Of course, sometimes they aggravate each other, and that always bothers me. I'm sure there is nothing that makes God happier than to see us (his children) loving each other. I'm equally sure that when we hurt each other, it breaks God's heart because God made us out of love and for love.

Love is so good that it must be true life as God meant it to be. If you doubt that, then consider the alternatives: hate, cruelty, hostility, indifference. These are all false; all are fake. These are all distortions of God's plan and God's truth. The truth is that God made us for love.

Second is humility. There is something very special, very Godlike, about the spirit of humility.

One of our Christian leaders, visiting in China, asked a group of Chinese pastors what it was in Christ that appealed most to them and won their hearts to him. None of them mentioned the miracles or even the Sermon on the Mount. One of the elders in a choking, faltering voice told the story of the upper room, of Christ taking a towel and washing the disciples' feet, becoming a humble servant.

Humility is so good that it must be life as God meant it to be. If you doubt that, then consider the alternatives: pompous pride, self-centered arrogance, egotistical acts, our shabby way of scrambling for the best seats. All of these are false, fake, phony. All are distortions of God's will for our lives. The truth is that God made us for love and humility.

Third is forgiveness. Forgiveness is another quality or spirit that is so special, so big, that it must be true. Look at Jesus on the cross and hear him saying: "Father, forgive them" (Luke 23:34). That is so good that it has to be authentic, it has to be of God.

Do you ever wonder, "Should I forgive that person who has wronged me or hurt me?" If that question ever comes to your mind, then just remember the picture of Jesus hanging on a cross saying, "Father, forgive them."

That is our measuring stick for forgiveness. That is the way God wants us to be. If you doubt that, then consider the alternatives: resentment, bitterness, vengeance. These are all false. All are distortions of God's will for our lives. The truth is that God made us for love, humility, and forgiveness. He showed us that on a cross!

Are You Dreaming the Impossible Dream?

Recently I visited with a man who was going through a middle years identity crisis. He was depressed. With a tone of despair, he lamented, "I've done nothing with my life! I'm a total zero! When I was young, I honestly thought I would one day be president of my company. I have not even come close, and I know now that I never will make it big. It's terribly painful for me to see what a loser I am!"

And yet, this man actually has made a fine record with his life. He has raised a wonderful family, has been a highly productive person for his company, has served effectively in the church, and has given strong leadership in his community. But now he is somehow despondent because there is no exotic moment of greatness in his life. He never realized his highest dreams. To him that feels like failure, and he sees himself as a loser. What do you think? Is he a failure? Is he a loser?

Not long ago, I heard a woman pour out her feelings about the untimely death of her husband. She said, "We had planned so carefully for our future, and had wanted such great things from our marriage, and now we have neither. We should have done so much more while we were still together. I really failed him!"

Well, the truth is, she had not failed him at all. They had the wonderful, vibrant kind of marriage that their friends sought to emulate. They had great children and rich memories, a wonderful home. Yet she said, "I failed him!"

A short time ago, a man spoke to me in similar fashion. He said, "My youth was filled with big dreams. I was going to be a professional athlete, a great one. And look at what happened. I ended up a middle-aged nothing!"

Well, I never thought of him as "a nothing." He made a good living for his family. He has been a devoted husband, an outstanding father, a conscientious citizen, and a fine churchman. In addition, he has given hours and hours to young people, coaching Little League, helping with school athletic events, working with the church youth program. Over the years, young people have admired him, learned from him, and loved him. Yet he had said, "I am a middle-aged nothing."

Now, when I think of these three persons, the thing that jumps out and strikes me most is this: only someone with great dreams can feel great disappointment.

And in that, these three people are very much like one of Jesus' earliest companions and closet friends: Simon Peter. Simon Peter experienced great disappointment—but only because he nourished such great dreams.

Very few biblical stories are charged with such dramatic power as that of the tense scene in which Peter denies his Lord three times. All four Gospel writers record it. What electricity is in this scene! Jesus has been arrested in the garden of Gethsemane and taken away. Peter follows. The scent of danger is in the air.

Jesus is falsely accused and brutally abused. They hit him, they slap him, they spit on his face. They mock him, they taunt him, they plot to crucify him.

And at that moment, they spot Simon Peter sitting outside in the courtyard. In that frightening hostile setting, they then begin to accuse Simon Peter. "Wait a minute! Were you with him? Yes, you. You were with Jesus. You are one of his followers!"

Afraid and confused (just like you and I would have been), Peter denies it! First he denied it with innocence. Later he denies it with an oath. And later still, he denies it with a curse!

Then—just then—the cock crows. Luke's Gospel has a penetrating sentence here. It's only in Luke, and it reads like this: "The Lord turned and looked straight at Peter" (Luke 22:61a).

How painful that must have been for Simon Peter. He remembered how he earlier had bragged of his commitment and loyalty and courage. And he remembered too how Jesus had said to him: "Before a rooster crows today, you will deny me three times" (Luke 22:61b).

Then Peter went out and wept bitterly.

At first glance, this looks like the story of failure. But as radio storyteller Paul Harvey would put it, we need to know "the rest of the story." As we keep on reading, we discover that no one ever learned better from failure than Simon Peter did. He was down, but not out. He made a great comeback! He picked up the dream again and with the help of God, made it a reality.

The rest of the story then is this: all the disciples ran out. They all fled. They all hid. They all failed Jesus. But when the dreaded events of that week were past and Easter dawned, it was Peter who rallied the others and became their strong leader.

He led them as together they dreamed an impossible dream.

Are You Locked in a Room with Open Doors?

Our own fears and weaknesses can cripple and shackle us. The truth is that we sometimes imprison ourselves by our own attitudes and fears. As Pogo put it in the comics, "We have met the enemy and he is us."

A dramatic, shocking illustration of this is found in disclosures about the last fifteen years of Howard Hughes's life. Hughes was a bashful and mysterious billionaire, a movie magnate, a daring aviator, an American hero, an untiring tinkerer who spurred science to new horizons.

A man of power, the envy of millions, he was in reality a self-inflicted prisoner, imprisoned by his own fears. A book about him called *The Hidden Years* shows Hughes in his last years as a tortured, troubled man who wallowed in self-neglect, lapsed into periods of near-lunacy, lived without comfort or joy in prison-like conditions, and ultimately died for lack of a medical device that his own foundation had helped to develop.

Time magazine, in its December 13, 1976, issue put it like this: "He was the world's ultimate enigma—man so secretive, so hidden from view that no outsider could say with certainty even whether he was alive, much less how he looked or behaved. He was one of the world's richest, most imperious, capricious, outrageous, eccentric and powerful men."

His physical appearance was horrifying. His straggly beard hung to his waist, his hair reached mid-back. His fingernails and toenails were more than two inches long. When he was still able, he walked with a pronounced stoop.

He actually had shrunk three inches and had lost weight down to a skeletal ninety pounds. He often went unclothed because he had grown afraid of buttons, zippers, and metal snaps. He suffered from anemia, arthritis, and assorted other ills and for the last six years of his life was completely unaware of the date, month, or even the season of the year.

He became so obsessed by fear of contamination from other human beings that he required his secretaries to wear white gloves to type any letter or memo that he would touch.

Howard Hughes, a man who had the means and power to do just about anything he wanted to do, existed in a self-made prison, a prison of his own choosing, a prison constructed of fear. He was locked in a room with open doors. He could have walked out, but he was afraid to do it.

In a different sense and on a different level, could this be true of us? It's not my purpose here to be critical of Howard Hughes. The point is, is his experience in those hidden years a parable for us? Do we have fears or attitudes or weaknesses that imprison us? Do crippling anxieties cut us off from life, from other people, from God?

Are we free, really free, to live fully as God intended? Or are we locked in a room with open doors? Listen to these poignant words written by a teenager:

> I want to touch you, world, but I'm afraid of being hurt and I'm afraid of being bitten and I'm afraid of being touched back—perhaps too deeply or too suddenly, and I will never be the same again. I want to touch you, world, but I'm afraid of reaching out too soon and I'm afraid of being left alone and I'm afraid of never knowing friendship and I'm afraid I'll lose my way and never find the safety of myself again. I want to touch you, world, and feel your pulse surge and hear your laughter and see your beauty and share your heartbeat and become a part of you. I want to touch you, world, but I don't want to leave my shell for it's far too safe and warm and soft in here and I don't know if I'm ready for you, yet. So let me test you world, please, just to see if there's a place in you for me.

How do we get out of the prison? Christ sets us free by showing us that "perfect love drives out fear" (1 John 4:18).

According to Alan Walker in *Jesus the Liberator*, this perfect love was witnessed in Marburg, Germany, when a mother lost sight of her daughter while at a circus. After searching, the mother was horrified to see that the child had somehow squeezed through the bars of the lion's cage and was next to the lion, which had bared its claws!

With no hesitation, the mother rushed through the door of the cage, grabbed the child in her arms, slammed the door in the lion's face, and promptly fainted.

That woman feared that lion as much as you and I would. But she is a mother. Her love for her endangered child cast out any sense of fear she might have had and sent her to do something, a risky something, that she would have thought impossible for her to do.

The point is clear. Love is the freeing agent, the deliverer. When love is strong enough, it will cast out fear and bring you out of whatever imprisons you.

Love sets us free to be God's children and God's stewards in the world.

Was the Innkeeper Really
a Bad Guy?

It was Christmas Eve in Bethlehem, Pennsylvania, in the 1990s. The innkeeper at the local Holiday Inn had had a busy day. It was late, and he was at the main desk alone. Although the inn was full with Christmas travelers, he had sent most of the workers home to be with their families for Christmas Eve, and the lobby was relatively quiet.

But as he was doing some paperwork at the front desk, he suddenly heard a noise and he looked up. He couldn't believe his eyes.

Walking in the main door of the Holiday Inn on this Christmas Eve in Bethlehem, Pennsylvania, was a young man wearing what looked to be an old tattered bathrobe while he was pulling a donkey behind him. On the donkey was a young woman who looked to be quite expectant. As they approached the desk, the young man announced, "My name is Joseph and this is Mary....And as you can see, she is about to have a baby. We need a room for the night." Before we get to the rest of the story, here is what was really happening that Christmas Eve in Bethlehem, Pennsylvania.

The young man's name was not really Joseph, and the young woman was not really named Mary. She was not expecting a baby. The young couple meant it to be a kind of political demonstration of the crass commercialization of Christmas.

Since there had been a "no vacancy" sign up for several hours, this modern-day Mary and Joseph fully expected to be turned away. They were certain they would be told that there was no room in the inn. Then their plan was to go to the news media with the story of their rejection.

But the innkeeper dealt them a surprise. Warmly, he rushed around the desk and welcomed them graciously:

"Mary and Joseph, you honor us by coming here tonight. What a privilege to have you under our roof! It's true that all of our regular rooms are taken, but we would be so pleased if you would occupy the bridal suite—and of course, there will be no charge."

That is what you call rising to the occasion. The innkeeper proved to be very wise. He knew the Christmas story, and he had something of the spirit of Christmas within him. He was also shrewd because he knew how harshly history can deal with an unsuspecting innkeeper.

Now that story jolted my conscience and made me look in a fresh, new way at the innkeeper in the original Christmas story. When we look at him with an open mind, several important and universal lessons about life stand up and stare us in the face. Let me suggest some of them.

One lesson is the danger of judging people or events without having all the facts. I rather suspect we have treated the innkeeper unfairly. History has dealt harshly with him. We have written him off as a bad character, harsh, irritable, insensitive, and uncaring, when the truth is we know virtually nothing about him. As a matter of fact, he is not even mentioned in the biblical accounts of the Christmas story. All Luke says is "no room in the inn," and out of those five words we have over the years performed a cruel character assassination.

The lesson is obvious. It is dangerous and destructive to judge people and events when we don't really know the situation or circumstances or facts. It can cause a lot of confusion and heartache.

A second lesson is that so often our choices are not so much between right and wrong or good and bad as between the lesser of two bad things. The innkeeper didn't have a good choice that night, but his decision may have been the best under the circumstances. He may well have been Mary and Joseph's best friend that night. Hotels in those days hardly were luxury accommodations. Most of them were two-story buildings. The upper floor was used for the guests (offering not much privacy) and the first floor was set aside for the animals upon which the people traveled. Hotels were cold, smelly places; and that night they were crowded and noisy— hardly a place for the birth of a baby.

But Bethlehem afforded another possibility. Built on a ridge of limestone, the town had numerous caves. Some of these caves were used as stables. They were not much better for an expectant mother, but at least there was warmth and quiet and some privacy.

If this is what happened on that night long ago, then our whole image of the innkeeper changes dramatically and we view him with kindness. Any decision he made was wrong. He could only choose the lesser of evils. We often face that kind of difficult decision and when we do, we have to prayerfully do the best we know and trust God to bring it out right.

A third lesson is that the real key in whatever you do is your attitude. It's not so much what we do as how we do it and why.

If, on the one hand, the innkeeper said to Mary and Joseph, "Get out of here. I'm full up and don't want to be bothered with you," then that's one thing. But if he said to them, "Look, my friends, all my spaces here are taken, but I know a place," then that's a different story, and the difference is in the attitude.

A fourth lesson is that God can redeem things. He can take defeats and turn them into victories. He can take a humble, lowly birth and make an asset out of it. He can take a cruel cross and make a triumph out of it.

This is the good news of our faith. God can take our blunders and mistakes and poor judgments and feeble efforts and redeem them and use them for good. He can work through us—and sometimes in spite of us.

Where's His?

Each year at Christmas, my mind darts back to a poignant Christmas story that I ran across some years ago.

It's about a woman, not rich and not poor, but whom God had blessed with a comfortable life and a comfortable family. She was putting the finishing touches on her Christmas tree and gifts for the family as she waited for her husband, who was working late on this Christmas Eve night.

She had finished the last ornaments on the tree and had gone over the long list of gifts for all those she was giving for Christmas to be sure she had not forgotten anyone. Finally, she said to herself, "Thank God, I believe this is one year I have remembered everyone and there will be no late Christmas Eve panic to go out and find that last-minute present for a forgotten relative or friend."

Then she sank back in a comfortable chair to relax a minute by the fireplace in front of the heavy-laden tree, and before she knew it she slept and dreamed. Suddenly there stood before her by the tree a small, thin, rather poorly dressed little girl.

Her large dark eyes looked with wonderment at the brightly decorated tree and the great pile of presents, and without taking her eyes off the tree she asked the lady, "What's that?"

The woman said, "That's my Christmas tree." For some reason she felt she should explain, and she said, "It's Christmas, you know."

The little girl said, "What's Christmas?"

"Why, don't you know? Christmas is Christ's birthday. This is the tree, and these are the Christmas presents. The red one over there is a hunting jacket for my husband, the big brown package is a game for my granddaughter, and the green one is for my son."

And over the huge pile of presents she named them one by one, making a special point not to leave out anyone. But when she finished, the little girl stood silently for a moment, looking over the presents as if searching for one not yet pointed out.

Then she said quietly, "Where's his?"

And, in her dream, suddenly the woman said, "Oh, have I forgotten someone? I thought this year I had remembered everyone on my list. Who have I forgotten?"

The little girl with the big, dark eyes replied, "You said Christmas is Christ's birthday. Where is his present?"

At that moment a car door slammed in the carport awaking the woman out of her dream. Her husband was home. When she opened her eyes, the little girl was gone and the Christmas tree lights twinkled, glistening off the brightly wrapped packages.

The little girl was gone, but her question remained, filling the whole room. And the woman hurriedly rose and went to let her husband in and to tell him about a visit from a little girl with large, dark eyes and the question she had asked and left to be answered.

It still remains to be answered, doesn't it? Where's his?

Will You Face Death Unafraid?

The great Christians were not afraid of death; they faced it squarely, confidently, and courageously. If life is Christ, then death will be more of Christ, and it will not be death at all but the entrance into a larger dimension of life with God. The great Christians have all been very sure of this. History records it over and over again.

On Sunday, April 8, 1945, Dietrich Bonhoeffer was condemned to death. Several accounts say he had been leading a worship service for his fellow prisoners in a Nazi concentration camp. Just as he finished his last prayer, the door flew open, and two powerful-looking men stepped inside. One of them shouted out, "Prisoner Bonhoeffer, come with us!" They all knew what it meant. Bonhoeffer was to be executed; he was to die. As Bonhoeffer walked out toward his fate, he said to his fellow prisoners, "This is the end, but for me the beginning of life." He was executed the next day.

Ignatius, the bishop of Antioch in the early Christian church, as he was led to the arena to be thrown to the lions said, "Grant me no more than to be a sacrifice for God while there is an altar at hand....I would rather die and get to Jesus Christ than reign over the ends of earth."

Polycarp, the bishop of Smyrna, was burned at the stake in the middle of the second century because he would not curse Christ and bow down to Caesar. According to Gene Fedele, before his accusers, Polycarp said, "Eighty-six years I have served Him. He has never done me wrong. How then can I blaspheme my King who has saved me?" Then as he died at the stake, he said a prayer of thanksgiving to God for the privilege of dying for the faith.

Susanna Wesley, mother of nineteen children, including John and Charles Wesley, on her deathbed called her children and their families to her side and said, "Children, as soon as I am released, sing a psalm of praise to God."

John Wesley's famous last words were words of great faith, "The best of all is, God is with us."

The Apostle Paul, as he faced death, spoke to his Philippian friends with a heart overflowing with joy. "Be glad in the Lord always! Again I say, be glad!...Because for me, living serves Christ and dying is even better" (Philippians 1:4, 21).

And we recall Jesus' confident words from the cross, "Father, into your hands I entrust my life."

Here we have a few examples of the witness of great men and women of faith facing death confidently and with deep faith and trust. Yet despite these courageous witnesses, and thousands more like them recorded in history, we have to be honest to admit that, more often than not, we would prefer not to think or talk about death.

Alexander Solzhenitsyn said, "Above all else, we have grown to fear death and those who die." But we need to know how to face the crisis of death and how to grieve productively and creatively. We don't really like to think of death, but we need to know how to handle it when someone we love dies. The most helpful thing is to remember that God is on both sides of the grave and that nothing—not even death—can separate us from him and his love.

Now, to underscore this, I could quote Jesus or Paul, but instead I will quote the words of a great scientist, Dr. Wernher von Braun, as he speaks on the subject, "Why I Believe in Immortality." He says,

> Many people seem to feel that science has somehow made such "religious ideas" [of immortality] untimely or old-fashioned. But I think science has a real surprise for the skeptics. Science tells us that nothing in nature, not even the tiniest particle, can disappear without trace....
>
> If God applies this fundamental principle to the most minute and insignificant parts of His universe, doesn't it make sense to assume that he applies it also to the masterpiece of His creation—the human soul?...Everything science has taught me...strengthens my belief in the continuity

of our spiritual existence after death. Nothing disappears without trace.

When someone you love dies, remember that! Remember that God is on both sides of the grave and nothing can separate us from him. God is there. That's really all we need to know!

Bibliography

Black, Christopher. "Tycoons: The Secret Life of Howard Hughes." *Time* (Dec. 13, 1976).

Fedele, Gene. *Heroes of the Faith: An Inspirational and Illustrated Account of 2,000 Years of Christianity*. Gainesville, FL: Bridge-Logos, 2003.

Fosdick, Harry Emerson. *Twelve Tests of Character*. New York: Harper & Brothers, 1923.

Gaddis, Thomas E., and Guy Trosper. *Birdman of Alcatraz*. Directed by John Frankenheimer. Starring Burt Lancaster. Beverly Hills: United Artists, 1962.

Gillies, Andrew. "The Two Prayers." In *Motives and Expression, in Religious Education: A Manual of Worship, Hand-Work, Play and Service*. By Charles S. Ikenberry. 1922. Reprint. London: Forgotten Books, 2013.

Hamilton, J. Wallace. *Where Now Is Thy God?* Grand Rapids: Revell, 1969.

Ignatius of Antioch. "Letter to the Romans." In *Callings: Twenty Centuries of Christian Wisdom on Vocation*. Edited by William Carl Placher. Grand Rapids: Eerdmans, 2005.

Kromer, Helen. "The Word." Pages 18–19 in *For Heaven's Sake! A Musical Revue in Two Acts*. Boston: Baker's Plays, 1961.

Phelan, James. *Howard Hughes: The Hidden Years*. New York: Random House, 1976.

Read, David Haxton Carswell. *Religion Without Wrappings*. Grand Rapids: Eerdmans, 1970.

Shedd, Charlie W. *Time for All Things*. Nashville: Abingdon, 1980.

Solzhenitsyn, Alexander. *Stories and Prose Poems*. Translated by Michael Glenny. New York: Farrar, Straus and Giroux, 1971.

von Braun, Wernher. "Personality of the Month." *Science of Mind* 40, no. 8 (August 1967): 107.

von Schlegel, Kathrina. "Be Still, My Soul." Translated by Jane L. Borthwick, 415. In *Christian Worship: A Lutheran Hymnal*. Milwaukee: Northwestern, 1993.

Walker, Alan. *Jesus the Liberator*. Nashville: Abingdon Press, 1973.

Wesley, Susanna. *Susanna Wesley: The Complete Writings*. New York: Oxford University Press, 1997.

Wilcox, Ella Wheeler. "The Winds of Fate." In *Masterpieces of Religious Verse*, edited by James Dalton Morrison, 314. New York and London: Harper & Brothers, 1948.